Button! Button!

Button! Button!

50 CUTE & CRAFTY PROJECTS

Terry Taylor

LARK BOOKS

A Division of Sterling Publishing Co., Inc.

New York / London

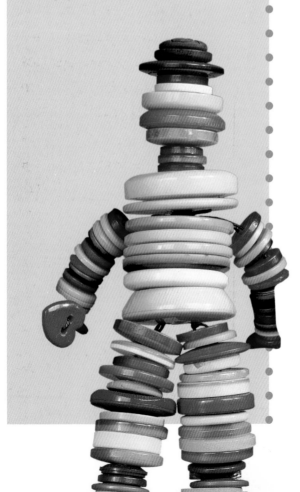

Editor: **Linda Kopp**

Art Director: **Kathleen Holmes**

Cover Designer: **Cindy LaBreacht**

Assistant Editors: **Mark Bloom, Julie Hale**

Editorial Assistance: **Dawn Dillingham, Amanda Wheeler**

Associate Art Director: **Avery Johnson**

Art Production Assistant: **Jeff Hamilton**

Photographer: **Stewart O'Shields**

Library of Congress Cataloging-in-Publication Data

Taylor, Terry, 1952-
    Button! button! / Terry Taylor.—1st ed.t
      p. cm.
    Includes index.
    ISBN-13: 978-1-60059-145-7 (pb-trade pbk. : alk. paper)
    ISBN-10: 1-60059-145-0 (pb-trade pbk. : alk. paper)
    1. Button craft. I. Title.
  TT880.T39 2008
  745.58'4—dc22

                2007028111

10 9 8 7 6 5 4 3 2 1
First Edition

Published by Lark Books, A Division of Sterling Publishing Co., Inc.
387 Park Avenue South, New York, NY 10016

Text © 2008, Lark Books
Photography © 2008, Lark Books unless otherwise specified

Distributed in Canada by Sterling Publishing, c/o Canadian Manda Group, 165 Dufferin Street
Toronto, Ontario, Canada M6K 3H6

Distributed in the United Kingdom by GMC Distribution Services, Castle Place, 166 High Street,
Lewes, East Sussex, England BN7 1XU

Distributed in Australia by Capricorn Link (Australia) Pty Ltd., P.O. Box 704, Windsor, NSW
2756 Australia

If you have questions or comments about this book, please contact:
Lark Books
67 Broadway
Asheville, NC 28801
828-253-0467

Manufactured in China

ISBN 13: 978-1-60059-145-7
ISBN 10: 1-60059-145-0

For information about custom editions, special sales, premium and corporate purchases, please
contact Sterling Special Sales Department at 800-805-5489 or specialsales@sterlingpub.com.

Introduction 6

Button Basics 8

Buttoned Up Accessories

Chichi Button Boutique 14

By the Sea Bag 16

Boho Silk Scarf 18

Electronic Gadget Cozy 20

Wheat Penny Buttons 23

Chic Shell Bag 26

Hair Ribbons 29

Cha-Cha Bracelet 30

Embellished Tote 33

At Home Slippers 34

Button Bedecked Bangles 36

Uptown Apron 38

Decoupage Buttons 40

Patchwork Pretties 43

Bird & Flower Brooches 46

The Button King 48

Buttons for House & Home

Cashmere Album Cover 51

Silhouette Lampshade 54

Vintage Memories Shadowbox 56

Midnight Sky Fleece Throw 58

Chinese Lantern 60

Fashion-Forward Desk Set 62

Celestial Glass Votives 64

Posy Pillows 66

Dem Bones, Dem Bone Buttons 68

Watch Me Bloom Toy Box 71

Charger Clock 74

Attractive Magnets 76

Freeform Embroidered Buttons 78

Oh-So-Casual Rug 81

Pyrographic Buttons 82

Snazzy Slipcover 85

Dishtowel Placemats 86

Celebratory Wreath 88

The Buttonarium 90

Button Whimsy

Confetti Wall Quilt 93

Buttoned-Down Cards 96

Clown Troupe 98

Toggle Button Seals 100

Keepsake Box Trio 102

Button-Bound Books 104

Adorned Scrapbook Pages 107

Simple Buttonhole Notecards 108

Elegant Packages 110

Baroque Holiday Tree 112

Wall Flowers 114

Button Monograms 116

Fanciful Bouquet 117

Big Button Pulls 120

Playful Tassels 122

Ribbon Bookmarks 124

Orb Ornaments 126

**Button Collecting
for Beginners** 128

**Warther Carving Museum
& Button Collection** 129

Designers 130

Index 132

Oh Button! Button!

Without a doubt, there's something about buttons that appeals to the child in each of us. Did you play in your grandmother's button box when you were a kid? You know, sorting piles of buttons according to their color and size? Do you find yourself drawn to buttons now, even though you're an adult? And do you purchase buttons even if you don't have a specific need for them?

If your answered "yes" to these questions, you're not alone. These days, the craft world is filled with buttonholics—folks who are unable to pass up browsing buttons no matter where they find them… in fabric shops, mass merchandisers, antique stores, or rummage sales. Buttons simply beckon to them like a charismatic circus hawker.

So just what is it about buttons that inspires obsession? The attraction is twofold. Obviously, they serve a practical purpose. On any given day you're bound to be wearing at least one. But buttons are also fun little works of art and can be the epitome of style, actually "making" an outfit.

If you've got bunches of buttons that you're yearning to use, or just want a good excuse to go on a button-shopping excursion, then *Button! Button!* is the book for you. You'll find 48 innovative, easy-to-make projects ranging from sophisticated accessories to whimsical housewares, all showcasing the classic little fasteners.

When it comes to crafting with buttons, anything goes: from the cozy At Home Slippers to the flirty Boho Silk Scarf, you'll find plenty of snazzy button-embellished wearables. Easy-to-assemble jewelry pieces, like the glittering Cha-Cha Bracelet and fanciful Bird & Flower Brooches, allow you to use buttons in ways you've never imagined! There are loads of button-covered creations for your home, ranging from classic to quirky—including a desk set and wall clock, pillows, placemats, magnets, and more. One of the great things about these projects—aside from their ingenious use of buttons—is that they're all beginner-friendly. Everything you need to know about materials and tools can be found in our basics chapter.

As you embark on these button-filled projects, don't be afraid to experiment. Try substituting buttons of different colors or materials for the ones used by the designers. You can easily customize each piece in this book, so that the finished products accent your décor and enhance your wardrobe.

See? We share your zeal and unabashedly embrace the button. Whoever coined the phrase "cute as a button" was a button lover for sure, and it's easy to see why. Buttons have never been fresher, more funky, or downright gorgeous than they are today. So select a project, break out the buttons, and get crafting.

BASICS

Anatomy of a Button

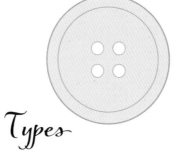

Types

Buttons come in an infinite variety of shapes, sizes, and colors. Here are the standard kinds you're most likely to encounter:

A **shank button** doesn't have a visible hole. Instead, it has a small ring or a bar with a hole called the shank protruding from the back of it, through which thread is sewn.

A **covered button** is a fabric-covered form with a separate back piece that secures the fabric over the knob.

A **flat** or **sew-through** button has two or four holes punched through it, through which the thread is sewn to attach the button.

A **worked** or **cloth button** consists of a knob or ring covered with embroidery or tight, crocheted stitches (usually of linen thread).

A **mandarin button** is a knob made of intricately knotted strings. In traditional mandarin dress (Qi Pao in Chinese), this type of button is closed with a loop. Pairs of mandarin buttons worn as cuff links are called silk knots.

A **ball-shaped button** has a hole drilled in it.

Sizes

Buttons are commonly measured in lignes (also called lines and abbreviated as "L"), with 40 lignes equal to 1½ inches (3.8 cm). Some standard sizes of buttons are 18L (11.43 mm, the standard button of men's shirts) and 32L (20.32 mm, a typical button on suit jackets).

Crafting Basics

As simple as sewing on a button: Yep, the projects in this book are that easy. You probably already have most of the craft materials required for putting together these projects. If you need a special tool—a certain size of hole punch, for instance, or a wood burning tool—it will be included in the materials list. Otherwise, you'll just need some basic tools and materials.

Button Toolbox

❏ Scissors
❏ Straight pins
❏ Sewing & embroidery needles
❏ Thread
❏ Embroidery floss
❏ Iron
❏ Ruler
❏ Pencil
❏ Paper
❏ Wire cutters
❏ Pliers
❏ File
❏ Adhesives

Types of Adhesives

All you do is glue it on: A dab of adhesive does the trick for attaching buttons to fabric, wood, or paper. Toothpicks are perfect for applying glue to the back of buttons, so be sure to keep some close by. Most of these projects call for some sort of glue, so here's a list of the types of sticky stuff you should have on hand:

❏ White craft glue
❏ Two-part epoxy
❏ Fabric glue
❏ Industrial strength glue
❏ Hot glue and a hot glue gun
❏ Spray adhesive
❏ Matte sealer/glue
❏ Glue stick

How to Sew on a Button

If you slept through Home Ec class, don't worry! Here's a refresher course in the simplest of sewing tasks.

Two-hole button

1. Cut 16 inches (40.6 cm) of thread and thread a needle. Use a double strand of thread.

2. Find the desired spot for the button.

3. Working from the wrong side of the fabric, poke the needle up through the spot. Pull it through until the knot sets.

4. Push the needle through the back of one hole; let the button fall to rest on the fabric.

5. Push the needle back down through the other hole and the fabric. Pull the thread until the button is tight against the cloth. Repeat several times, sewing in the same direction.

6. Bring the needle up through the fabric (but not through the button). Wind the thread under the button a

On the Button

Buttons have been a fashion staple for centuries. Here's a bit of background on the indispensable little notion.

The word *button* comes from the Old French term *bouton*, which means bud or knob.

The button was invented in Asia thousands of years ago. Ornamental buttons dating back to 2000–1500 BC have been discovered in China and the Middle East.

During the 16th century, France was the international capital of the button industry. French monarch Francis I had a costume covered with 13,600 buttons. Frenchmen sported buttons adorned with the portraits of their favorite ladies.

Eighteenth-century buttons had anywhere from three to five holes. It wasn't until the early nineteenth century, when manufacturers started machine-drilling buttons instead of producing them by hand, that the two- and four-hole types became standard.

A laborer in a button factory in the early 1900s could turn out about 3,300 buttons per day. Plastic molding machines, introduced around the same time, could produce 5,000 buttons per minute.

In years past, manufacturers used natural materials like bone or shell to hand-produce buttons. Today, just about any material imaginable can be used to make buttons, including antler, celluloid, glass, horn, ivory, metal, paste, plastic, pearl, porcelain, vegetable ivory, and wood.

few times, and then poke the needle back to the wrong side of the fabric. Make a knot to secure the thread, then cut off any excess.

Four-hole button

1. Follow the instructions for a two-hole button above, but use twice as much thread.

2. Start sewing from one hole to the one beside it; after you've repeated this several times, repeat on the other pair of holes to create two lines of parallel stitching. (While parallel lines look more professional, you can

also sew in an X or in a square. Any of these methods holds the button securely.)

Shank-back button

1. Secure the thread with a knot and then push the needle through the back of the fabric. Stab the needle through the shank. Push the needle back down through the right side of the fabric ¹⁄₁₆ inch (1.6 mm) from the incoming thread. Make sure the shank lies where you want it before continuing.

2. Pull the thread until the button is tight against the fabric. Repeat several times, sewing in the same direction. On the wrong side of the fabric, make a knot to secure the thread, and trim the excess thread.

Tools of the Trade

Wire cutters are perfect for snipping shanks off metal buttons, while a file works well for removing shanks from plastic buttons. A number of projects call for the standard types of pliers—chain-nose, round-nose, and flat-nose—so be sure to round them up before you begin.

Buttoned Up Accessories

Terry Taylor

Chichi Button Boutique

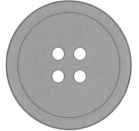

Have you ever fallen deliriously in love with a pair of buttons and then racked your brain trying to figure out what to do with them? Buy some jewelry findings and fashion your beloved buttons into a pair of arty boutique earrings.

2 buttons

Ear posts, hoops, or ear wires

Drill and drill bit (optional)

Seed beads (optional)

Pliers

Wire cutters

File

Select your buttons. The backs of flat buttons are perfect for mounting posts. Shank buttons can be easily suspended on ear wires or hoops.

Glue the posts to the flat backs of a pair of buttons. If you purchase posts with pads, simply mix up a small amount of two-part epoxy following the manufacturer's instructions, and adhere them to the buttons. Posts without pads require that you drill a tiny depression slightly smaller than the diameter of the post. Mix up the epoxy, place a small amount in the depression, and set the post in the depression.

Slip a single, stunning shank button onto a hoop, or thread on several buttons interspersed with seed beads. Using pliers, form the catch by turning up the end of the wire hoop.

Cut off the shank of a button if you prefer to wear posts. Wire cutters will easily cut metal shanks. Use a file to get rid of a shank on plastic buttons. Simply file the shank until it is flush with the back of the button, then adhere an ear post.

Joan K. Morris

By the Sea Bag

A towel, sunblock, the latest best seller…going to the beach or lake requires the proper gear. Carry everything you need in a generous straw tote embellished with buttons arranged in nautical themes.

Assorted blue buttons, ¼ to 1 inch (6 mm to 2.5 cm) (The number of buttons needed will depend on the size of your design.)

White straw tote bag, 16 x 12 inches (40.6 x 30.5 cm)

1½ yards (1.4 m) of blue grosgrain ribbon, ½ inch (1.3 cm) wide

Arrange the buttons on the bag according to the designs in the project photo.

Glue the buttons in place carefully using small dabs of fabric glue on the back of each button. Try not to cover the button holes with glue. Let dry for about 20 minutes.

Use embroidery floss to stitch each button in place, or permanently glue them to the bag using industrial strength glue, following the manufacturer's instructions. Make sure the tote is lying flat while the glue dries.

Hot-glue the ½-inch-wide (1.3 cm) ribbon around the top inside rim of the tote, after all the buttons are sewn in place.

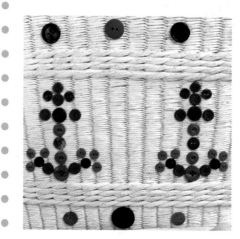

Boho Silk Scarf

What's black and white and red all over? Why, this artfully textured scarf. Oh-so-sheer fabric scraps are stacked and stitched, then crowned with a bejeweled button.

¼ yard (.23 m) of black silk chiffon,

Silk chiffon in red, cream with polka dots, and cream with a black pattern, ⅛ yard (.11 m) each

⅛ yard (.11 m) of cream netting

Multi-needle felting tool

Large needle felting mat

Silk chiffon scarf

Sewing machine

20 black buttons, each ⅜ inch (9.5 mm)

3 cream buttons, each ⅜ inch (9.5 mm)

16 cream buttons, each ½ inch (1.3 cm)

Cut 3 x 2-inch (7.6 cm x 5 cm) rectangles and 2-inch (5 cm) squares from each of the chiffon and netting fabrics.

Distress and fray the fabric squares and rectangles, laying them on the needle felting mat and punching them with a multi-needle tool until you achieve the desired effect. You can also unravel the edges by pulling away some of the threads around the border.

Lay the scarf out lengthwise on a table, then stack and arrange the rectangles and squares as desired or as shown in the project photo. When you're satisfied, pin them in place. Remember to alternate the squares and rectangles.

Use a sewing machine to stitch the stacks to the scarf. Leave a large seam allowance if you want the frayed edges. You can stitch around each piece of fabric in the stack or all of them together.

Lay out a button (or buttons) on top of each rectangle, using the photos or your own design. Hand-stitch the buttons to secure them in place.

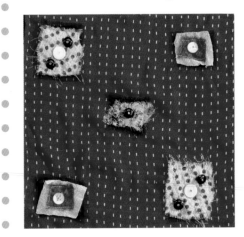

Candie Cooper

Elizabeth Hooper

Electronic Gadget Cozy

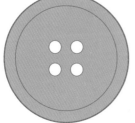

Love your mp3? Can't imagine life without your cell phone? Protect your electronic goodies with a soft and stylish felt case customized with either a few or a bunch of buttons.

Felt in several colors

Embroidery needle

Embroidery floss in several matching or contrasting colors

Assorted buttons

NOTE: the finished cozys pictured are about 3¼ x 4½ inches (8.3 x 11.4 cm) and fit the standard iPod or video iPod. It also fits some digital cameras and cell phones.

Create a paper pattern by tracing around your electronic device. Add ¼ inch (6 mm) to all the sides.

Use the pattern to cut the following 4 rectangular pieces from the felt: 1 piece for the front of the cozy, 1 piece for the back, and 2 separate pieces for the lining. (You can use one color for all the rectangles, or use an alternating color for a contrasting lining.)

Cut out one smaller rectangle in a color that contrasts with the front of the cozy. If you're making a cozy with felt circles, cut out the appropriate number of circles in a color that contrasts with the smaller rectangle.

Place the smaller, contrasting rectangle on the top of one of the larger rectangles, using the project photo as a guide. Position the contrasting rectangle about ½ inch (1.3 cm) from the left edge, then stitch down both sides with embroidery floss. Trim the piece along the top and bottom edges after stitching. This piece will serve as the front of the cozy.

Electronic Gadget Cozy

Stitch the circles onto the piece using matching thread, if you're making a design with felt circles. Embellish with buttons, or make a collage on the smaller rectangle with different buttons.

Sew a lining piece to the back of the front piece, and sew the other lining piece to the inside of the back piece of the cozy.

Place the two pieces of the cozy together and top-stitch along the outside edge by hand, burying the knots in the inside of the two pieces.

Wheat Penny Buttons

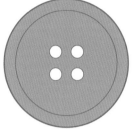

Get your money's worth with these buttons. Inspired by buttons created by Navajo silversmiths in the late 19th and early 20th centuries, they add a touch of refinement, and don't require soldering skills.

Wheat pennies*

Awl or nail

Drill and small drill bit

Abrasive pad

*Wheat pennies were minted from 1909 to 1958 and contain 95% copper and 5% of a mixture of tin and zinc. Pennies minted after 1982 contain 97.5% zinc and 2.5% copper plating. You'll see a difference in color when you drill into modern pennies.

Wheat Penny Buttons

Shine your pennies if they're tarnished. There are a variety of methods for shining them: try commercial metal polishes, soak the pennies in a mixture of salt and vinegar, or clean them with toothpastes or hot sauces!

Use the awl or sharp nail to mark points for two or four holes in your buttons.

Create the holes using a small drill bit. Don't press too hard with the drill bit in an effort to drill the holes in a hurry. That will heat up the penny, making it difficult to hold securely, as well as wear out the bit. If needed, use the abrasive pad to remove any burrs on the back of the drilled holes.

Stitch the buttons to your material with matching thread, or throw caution to the wind and use a coppery metallic thread instead. The thread may not stand up well to hard use, but it will be pretty!

Terry Taylor

Chic Shell Bag

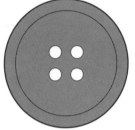

Fashion divas will tell you that accessories make the outfit. With the help of iridescent shell buttons you can create a stunning evening bag fit for any special occasion.

Beading and sharp sewing needles

Color coordinating beading thread

Beeswax

Purchased black fabric evening bag (one you can easily stitch buttons to)

Shell buttons in various colors and sizes*

E–beads, in coordinating color mix, approximately 30 grams

½ yard (.4 m) satin ribbon, ⅜ inch (9.5 mm) wide (optional)

*½-inch, ⅝-inch, ¾-inch, and ⅞-inch (1.3 cm, 1.6 cm, 1.9 cm, and 2.2 cm) are used in the bag shown in the project photo. The total number of buttons you'll need depends on the size of your bag and how densely you place the buttons. The bag used for this project is approximately 5½ x 11 inches (14 x 27.9 cm), which required about 400 buttons.

Thread the needle with a doubled length of beading thread, then wax the thread with beeswax. Knot the thread at the end and stitch into the bag fabric—you can start anywhere. Keep the knots on the front of the bag; you'll cover them with buttons so they won't show. For lined bags, be careful not to catch the lining fabric. No threads should show inside the bag.

Bring the threaded needle through one of the buttonholes, from back to front. Add a bead onto the thread and insert the needle through the other buttonhole. Stitch into the bag fabric and tighten so the bead and button are close to the bag. Stitch through the button and bead twice more to make sure they're securely attached.

Stitch into the bag fabric and bring the needle out a short distance away from the first button. Sew on another button and bead. Depending on the desired effect, you can sew the buttons to overlap, covering the bag's fabric completely, or you can use fewer buttons, allowing the bag fabric to show. Or, you may choose to cover just the front of the bag.

Elaine Schmidt

Chic Shell Bag

Vary the colors and sizes of the buttons as you sew buttons and beads onto the bag. You can sew small buttons onto large buttons for a layered effect (see the project photo).

OPTIONAL: If the bag has a handle, you can remove it and thread satin ribbon through the bag handle hardware.

QUICK & EASY

Hair Ribbons

Enhance a casual or formal hairstyle with an ornament that you can create in minutes.

Thread and then center a ribbon or sturdy thread through the shank of a button.

Slip a bobby pin through the shank and use the ribbon to tie a firm knot around it.

Diane Baker

Cha-Cha Bracelet

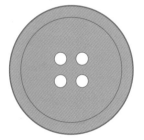

Are you feeling carefree and playful or after-five elegant? Whatever your mood, these bracelets have got you covered. Multitudes of buttons and beads jostling one another on a simple link bracelet create the effect.

Assortment of buttons in selected color palette, ⅜ to 1 inch (9.5 mm to 2.5 cm)

Approximately 20 silver eye pins, 2 inches (5 cm) long (choose an assortment of loop sizes)

Flat-nose pliers

Approximately 130 base metal head pins, 2 inches (5 cm) long

Chain-nose pliers

Round-nose pliers

Approximately 300 assorted beads in selected color palette, 2 mm to 10 mm

Wire cutters

Cha-Cha bracelet form, 15 mm

Attach buttons to the eye pins before attaching them to the bracelet form. To attach buttons with shanks to the eye pins, use flat-nose pliers to open up a loop on one of the eye pins, then slide the shank onto the pin and close the loop. Use the flat-nose pliers to bend the end of each head pin to a 45° angle just above the button shank, then use the wire cutters to trim the wire so that ⅜ inch (9.5 mm) remains, and finish the end with a loop.

Candie Cooper

Cha-Cha Bracelet

Open up an eye pin and thread the button onto the loop. Wiggle the loop end of the wire through and then close it. If the eye pin's loop is too small, you may have to make your own larger loop with the round-nose pliers. Finish the end with a loop as in the previous step.

String the beads onto the head pins. Repeat for the desired number of beaded head pins. Finish each end with a loop.

Open each loop with the flat-nose pliers and connect it to a loop on the bracelet's band bar, adding beaded head pins and buttons to the bracelet as desired.

TIP: Make beaded head pins in a variety of lengths using one or more beads. Work around the large focal buttons to create continuity. If you have empty spaces, string some of the small beads onto the head pins to create filler.

Embellished Tote

With just a few buttons and stitches you can transform a plain Jane tote into a trendy fashion accessory.

Terry Taylor

Purchase a simple tote and stitch or glue a handful of buttons down the front.

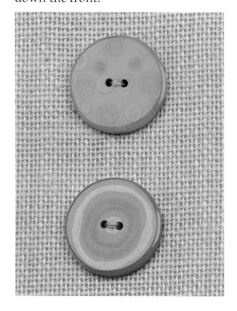

Candie Cooper

At Home Slippers

At the end of the day when you shed your office attire, pair your loungewear with a pair of kicky little slipper mules. They make a snazzy fashion statement, even with a pair of sweats and a T-shirt!

100% wool sweater or wool felt (for fringe)

Purchased slippers

60 assorted buttons

Two 12-inch (30.5 cm) pieces of velvet rickrack or trim, each ⅜ inch (9.5 mm) wide

NOTE: Your slippers will be different from the ones shown, so adjust widths, lengths, and quantities as needed when embellishing.

Make the felt trim either by felting a wool sweater in your washing machine or by purchasing ready-made wool felt.

Cut two 1½ x 12-inch (3.8 x 30.5 cm) strips of felt, then snip slits along the lengths to create a fringe. Pin the felt fringe in place on the slippers and then use a straight stitch to secure the trim to the slippers.

Stitch buttons to the slippers until you are satisfied with the appearance.

Glue the rickrack on top of the fringe using fabric glue. Before gluing down the ends, fold each under for a neat, finished look. Use straight pins to hold the trim in place while it dries.

Terry Taylor

Button Bedecked Bangles

These felted bangles beg to be bedecked with the tiniest of buttons. Bet you'll want to create an armload of these stylish bracelets.

Commercially made felt bangles*

Small buttons

* If you can't find similar bangles, it isn't difficult to felt your own bracelet. You can adapt this project by stitching buttons onto felted beads purchased at your local bead store. Simply string the felt beads on an elastic cord, knot the cord, and you've got a bracelet.

Use a doubled thread to stitch on the buttons. Knot the end. Give the thread a bit of a tug to pop the knot into the felted bangle.

Stitch buttons around the outer edge of the bracelet first. Bring the needle through the bracelet to the edge. Make a tiny stitch, then bring the thread up through a button and back down into the bracelet. Pass the needle to the inside of the bracelet and out the opposite side. Continue around the bracelet, anchoring the thread with a small stitch before attaching the button.

Stitch buttons to the top and bottom of the bracelet once you've created a line of buttons on the outer edge. Be sure you anchor each button with a small stitch.

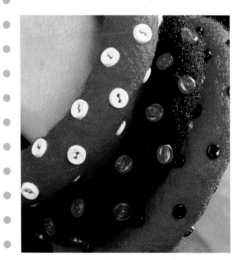

Uptown Apron

Aprons are back in vogue, but many show no resemblance to their '50s and '60s housewife-era kin. Trade in that Kiss the Cook apron for this beaded beauty. With its swags and tassels of buttons, it's a shame to keep this apron in the kitchen.

Purchased black apron

2 white buttons, each 1 inch (2.5 cm)

5 white buttons, each ¾ inch (1.9 cm)

85 small white buttons

Toothpick (to apply glue)

Place the apron on a flat surface and position the buttons on the apron as shown in the project photo or in your desired pattern.

Use fabric glue to attach each button. Let dry for 20 minutes.

Stitch each button in place.

Joan K. Morris

Terry Taylor

Decoupage Buttons

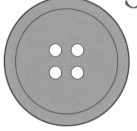

Decoupage is a quick and clever way to create decorative buttons. You can choose from a seemingly endless array of colored and patterned papers to match any outfit or décor.

Wood shapes

Awl or small nail

Tiny screw eyes

Acrylic paint and brush

Decorative papers*

Decoupage medium and brush

Acrylic varnish

*Use thin, flexible papers for best results. Handmade Asian papers and tissue papers are a delight to work with. Use either patterned or plain papers as desired.

Pierce the backside of the wood shape with the awl or the nail. Twist in a small screw eye to create a shank button. The screw eye makes a perfect little handle for you to hold as you paint or decoupage the button.

Decoupage Buttons

Paint the wood buttons with the acrylic paint. Be sure you paint both sides. Allow the painted surfaces to dry. If you're in a hurry, you can speed up the drying process with a hairdryer!

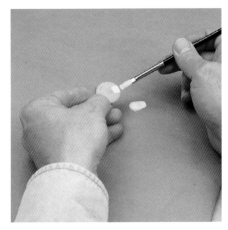

Cut or tear the decorative papers into small pieces. Adhere the paper to the painted surfaces with a thin coat of the decoupage medium. If desired, add decorative accents such as vintage paper clippings or other patterned papers. Allow the buttons to dry overnight. If the buttons are going to receive a lot of wear and tear, give them a protective coat of acrylic varnish after they have dried thoroughly.

Patchwork Pretties

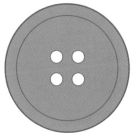

Why settle for simple cloth-covered buttons when you can create one-of-a-kind patchwork buttons? Make the patchwork with matching or contrasting fabrics—the choice is yours.

3 different fabric strips

Rotary cutter (optional)

Sewing machine*

Self-covering button forms

*It's a snap to stitch up patchwork using a sewing machine, but you can also hand stitch with a needle and thread.

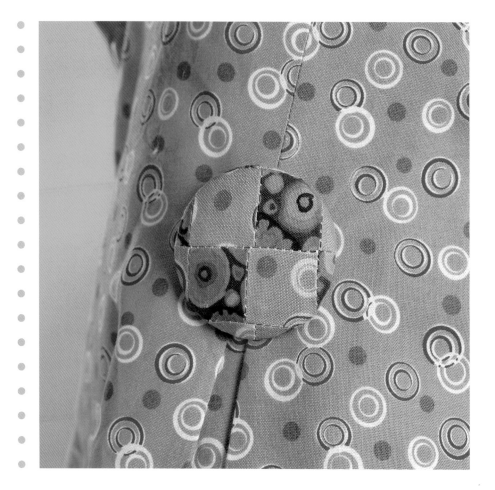

Patchwork Pretties

Cut three different fabrics into 1 x 12-inch (2.5 x 30.5 cm) strips. Scissors work just fine, but a rotary cutter makes the job go faster.

Stitch the strips together using a ⅜-inch (9.5 mm) seam, keeping right sides together. Press the seams open with the iron after you stitch them.

Cut the three stitched strips into rectangles approximately 1½ (3.8 cm) inches wide. Arrange the rectangles, alternating the fabric colors to create a checkerboard effect. Stitch the rectangles together using ⅜-inch (9.5 cm) seams. Press the seams open.

Follow the manufacturer's instructions to cover the button forms.

Terry Taylor

Sandy Snead

Bird & Flower Brooches

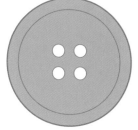

Flower buttons blooming on a felt background highlight a pair of whimsical brooches. Petite bugle beads or a couple of embroidery stitches add the finishing touch.

Bezel, 40 x 30 mm

Felt

Fleece

Large flower- or bird-shaped button

6-strand embroidery floss in two coordinating colors

Small beads (optional)

One-piece pin back

Use the bezel as a template to cut out a piece of felt and a piece of fleece. The fleece will provide padding and give depth to the brooch—it won't be visible, so the color you choose is optional.

Place the felt piece on top of the fleece piece. Hold the two pieces together tightly, and then sew the decorative button onto the front of the felt. To keep the button from moving as you sew, apply a small amount of matte sealer/glue to the underside of the button, adhering it to the fabric.

Cut out leaf shapes from the felt and stitch into place, if desired.

Divide one color of the embroidery floss into three strands, and use it to sew a running stitch around the inside edge of the fabric.

Divide the second color of embroidery floss into three strands, and use it to stitch around the edge of the fabric again, in between the running stitch. If you like, add small beads or stitch French knots.

Apply a thin-to-medium coat of matte sealer/glue to the bottom and inside edges of the bezel. Place the finished piece in the bezel, pressing it lightly into place. Use industrial strength glue to attach a pin back to the upper half of the bezel.

The Button King

Bishopville, South Carolina

Some people count sheep to try and fall asleep, but that never worked for Dalton Stevens. A long-time insomniac, Dalton turned his attention to buttons. After a string of sleepless nights back in 1983, Dalton started sewing buttons onto a denim suit. After two years, ten months and countless all-nighters, Dalton completed the suit with 16,333 buttons! It weighed 16 pounds and became the ultimate uniform for the man now famously known as "The Button King."

Dalton continued his late-night hobby by counting out and gluing 3,005 buttons on a guitar and 517 buttons on a pair of shoes. He went to the local newspaper, which lead to a write-up and a TV appearance on CNN, where his story was broadcast to the world. After a visit from Star Magazine, Dalton was summoned to appear on the Tonight Show with Johnny Carson, David Letterman, and Regis and

Kathy Lee, among other shows. His art form proved to be a bona fide hit—no ifs, ands, or buttons!

Although many people consider insomnia a curse, Dalton claims sleeplessness was the driving force behind his button craft, and all the recognition and rewards that have followed. "I believe I've been blessed in life to be able to do something that seems meant to be," he states on his website. "I got the chance to visit and entertain people in places I never would have gotten to if it hadn't been for the insomnia causing me to put buttons on items."

Sometimes going as long as four or five days without sleep, Dalton has completely covered two cars in buttons (one is his Button Hearse that will take him on his final lap), in addition to several more suits, a commode, and a coffin in which he intends to be buried.

To see more photos of Dalton Stevens and his work, visit www.scbuttonking.com.

Buttons for House & Home

Cashmere Album Cover

A simple cloth cover can dress up and protect a cherished photo album. Join distinctive buttons and patchwork fabric squares to form a pleasing checkerboard design.

6 textural materials,
¼ yard (.2 m) each

Sewing machine

Cashmere and coordinating
thread, 1 yard (.9 m) each

16 buttons

Scrapbook with 12 x 12-inch
(30.5 x 30.5 cm) pages

Silver shank button

½ yard (.5 m) of ribbon, ⅝ inch
(1.6 cm) wide, with matching
thread

Seam sealant

NOTE: When stitching fabric together, leave a ¼- inch (6 mm) seam allowance. Always press your seams open.

- **Cut** the six ¼-yard materials into sixteen 3-inch (7.6 cm) squares.

Cashmere Album Cover

Lay out the squares (four across by four down) in the desired arrangement. Pin and stitch the horizontal rows together first, then pin and stitch the finished rows together so that each of the four corners meets up. Set the patchwork piece aside.

Cut two strips of the cashmere, one 10½ x 6¾ inches (26.7 x 17.1 cm) and the other 10½ x 3¾ inches (26.7 x 9.5 cm). Pin the larger strip to the right side of the patchwork piece, right sides together, and stitch. Repeat with the smaller piece on the left side.

Cut two 2 x 20-inch (5 x 50.8 cm) cashmere strips. Pin and stitch them to the top and bottom of the patchwork piece.

Cut a 13½ x 18-inch (34.3 x 45.7 cm) rectangle from the cashmere. Stitch it to the left side of the patchwork piece for the back cover.

Stitch a button to the middle of each square. Split the floss in half and use two strands to make a diagonal stitch in the corner of each square. Tie the ends into a knot and leave the tails long.

Cut the lining fabric into a 38 x 13½-inch (96.5 x 34.3 cm) rectangle. Pin the two pieces, right sides together, leaving a 4-inch (10.2 cm) opening. Stitch all the way around. Turn the piece right side out through the opening and press. Hand-stitch the opening closed.

Wrap the cover around the outside of the book and fold the extra 4 inches (10.2 cm) on both ends to the inside. Pin the flaps in place along the sides and hand-stitch along the top and bottom edges.

Stitch on the silver button, using the project photo as a guide for placement.

Fold the ribbon over ¼ inch (6 mm) and press. Stitch it onto the back cover. Cut the end of the ribbon at an angle and seal with seam sealant.

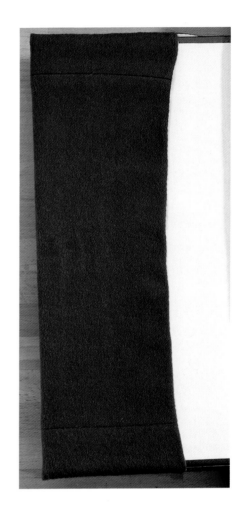

Candie Cooper

Silhouette Lampshade

By the light of day this plain lampshade appears to have only a soupcon of buttons along the edge. But at night, a striking graphic pattern of buttons appears at the flip of a switch.

Black craft paper

Circle punches*

Purchased shade

Buttons

*Use a variety of sizes, from large to small, as well as a handheld punch.

NOTE: Because the silhouettes inside the shade are paper, use a maximum 40-watt bulb in the lamp.

Use the black paper to cut out "buttons" in a variety of sizes. Use a handheld punch to create the holes in the buttons. Spray the "buttons" with adhesive and adhere them to the inside of the shade. Smooth them in place with your fingers. Use a hot glue gun to hot-glue the real buttons to the lower edge of the shade. In the lampshade shown in the project photo, buttons of different sizes were used to create a subdued pattern.

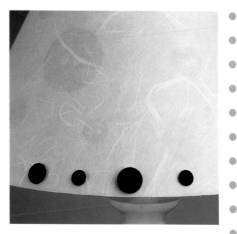

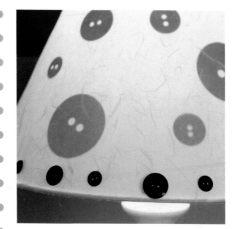

Joan K. Morris

Vintage Memories Shadowbox

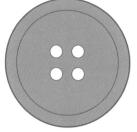

Don't leave Great-Grammy's photos languishing in a shoebox—use a shadowbox to display and protect them at the same time. To heighten the nostalgic setting, select buttons with the same tonal feel and sprinkle them throughout the arrangement.

Sheet of decorative paper, 8½ x 11 inches (21.6 x 27.9 cm)

Shadowbox, 9 x 9 x 3 inches (22.9 x 22.9 x 7.6 cm)

1-inch (2.5 cm) paintbrush (for decoupage)

Old photographs (or copies)

Card stock

Vintage or antique-looking buttons

Lace and satin ribbon (optional)

Slide out the panel and glass to allow you access to the inside of the shadowbox. Cut the decorative paper to cover all the inside surfaces of the shadowbox. Attach using decoupage glue.

Cut out the photos and glue them onto the card stock with a glue stick.

Stitch buttons around the photos.

Use the glue stick to attach the lace, vintage buttons, ribbon, and photos as desired, looking at the project photo as a guide for placement.

Secure heavier items (like the buttonhook) with a few well-placed stitches through the shadowbox backing.

Reassemble the shadowbox.

Midnight Sky Fleece Throw

Like stars winking in the night sky, metal buttons are scattered across a cozy polar fleece throw. Alternating scallops are studded to provide additional interest.

Scalloped-edged fleece throw

120 silver beads,
each ¼ inch (6 mm)

120 silver buttons,
each ½ inch (1.3 cm)

Use the straight pins to mark the places where you want the buttons and the beads sewn on, working with one quarter of the throw at a time.

Stack a bead on top of a button and sew both securely to the throw. Hide the knots under the buttons.

Joan K. Morris

Joan K. Morris

Chinese Lantern

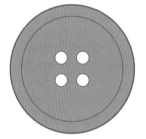

You don't have to wait until the Chinese New Year to break out the paper lanterns. In keeping with the organic tone, triangles of abalone and big wooden buttons are stitched onto tissue paper using lengths of raffia.

20 triangle shell buttons, each ¾ inch (1.9 cm)

20 round wooden buttons in assorted sizes, each 1 to 1½ inches (2.5 to 3.8 cm)

Paper lantern shade, 12 inches square (30.5 cm)

Clear shipping tape

Raffia

Large-eyed sewing needle (large enough for raffia)

Decide where you want to place the buttons on the lantern, and lightly mark those areas with a pencil.

Cut ¾-inch (1.9 cm) squares of clear shipping tape and place the squares over the pencil marks, on both the outside and the inside of the shade.

Cut a length of raffia and thread it through the needle. Thread the needle and raffia through one of the shell buttons and then through one of the wooden buttons. Run the raffia through a taped area on the shade from front to back, then back through the shade and buttons to the front. Tie a knot in the raffia to hold the buttons in place.

Place another piece of the clear tape on the inside of the shade, covering the other piece of tape and the raffia. Repeat these steps with all the buttons on all four sides of the shade.

Fashion-Forward Desk Set

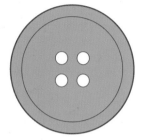

Gone are the days of the plastic pencil cup. Banish those drab office supply holders! Your desk will be stylin' when you spice up ordinary mesh accessories with color-coordinated buttons.

Wire mesh desk accessory

Skein of embroidery floss in a coordinating color

#2 crewel embroidery needle

Waxed linen thread

Large round buttons (35 mm was used)

Small round buttons (10 mm was used)

Medium round buttons (25 mm was used)

Find the center seam where two pieces of mesh overlap. Thread a needle with a 24-inch (61 cm) length of the embroidery floss that's knotted at one end. Baste a line down the length of the seam, making 1 to 2 inch stitches. The stitches will aid in the placement of the buttons.

Make additional rows of basting stitches at regularly spaced intervals, taking the size of your buttons and your desk accessories into account.

Thread the needle with a 24-inch (61 cm) piece of the waxed linen, making a large enough knot at the end so that it won't pull through the mesh when you stitch. Starting with the center seam (note that the letter box doesn't have a seam), sew on a line of buttons, alternating largest with the smallest, being careful not to stitch through the floss. When you reach the top, tie off your thread inside, and knot it.

Alternate button sizes as shown in the project photos, continuing to stitch on buttons in the same fashion around the outside of each accessory. As you're stitching, carefully cut the floss and pull it out of the holes.

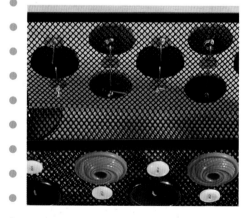

Andrea L. Stern

Skip Wade

Celestial Glass Votives

Like suspended shards of shimmering ice, glass buttons weave a mesmerizing dance around a simple cylinder.

Flat-face buttons

Glass vase

Wire cutters

24-gauge steel wire

Glue the flat-face buttons to the vase with cyanoacrylate glue, positioning the buttons randomly around the vase.

Use the wire cutters to cut a 12-inch (30.5 cm) piece of the steel wire. Insert the wire through the holes in one of the unattached buttons, twisting it tightly at the back of the button. Then thread the wire through one of the attached buttons and pull the wire so that the new button sits on top of the fixed button. Thread two to four additional buttons onto the wire, about an inch apart, twisting the wire tightly at the back of the final button.

Cut another 12-inch (30.5 cm) piece of the wire and thread it through another fixed button, bending the wire to fill the space between the two fixed buttons. Repeat these steps until the desired coverage on the vase is achieved.

Terry Taylor

Posy Pillows

These pillows are not your garden-variety florals. Simple punched felt shapes are embellished with buttons and scattered on luscious chocolate brown felt.

½ yard (.5 m) brown felt

Punched felt shapes*

Buttons

Sewing machine

Square pillow form, 14 inches (35.6 cm)

*The felt shapes shown were purchased. If you wish to make your own, use a decorative punch to cut out the shapes. Back a piece of felt with copy paper and punch out the shape.

Cut out one 18-inch (45 cm) square of brown felt for the front of the pillow.

Cut out two 18 x 11-inch (45.7 x 27.9 cm) rectangles of brown felt for the back of the pillow.

Create an 18-inch (45.7 cm) square by overlapping the two rectangles of brown felt. Pin the two rectangles together in the center and set it aside.

Mark a 15-inch (38.1 cm) square with a light-colored pencil, centered on the 18-inch (45.7 cm) square.

Arrange the felt shapes as desired inside the marked square. When you are satisfied with the design, adhere the shapes to the felt with a small amount of fabric glue or fusible webbing.

Machine-stitch buttons in the center of each felt shape. Then place the button-bedecked square on top of the overlapped rectangles.

Stitch along the marked lines on the top square, backstitching at the beginning and end of your stitching line.

Slip the pillow form between the overlapped edges on the back of the pillow cover.

Dem Bones, Dem Bones Buttons

Bone—the plastic of its day—was once a common button material. These vintage bone buttons acquired a lovely patina over time. Once used to button nightshirts, uniforms, or work clothes, in this pair of projects they're employed in a more elegant way.

BASKETS

Cut a length of copper wire. Fold the wire in half over a pencil or your finger to create a U-shape.

Create a graduated stack of bone buttons, starting by threading the two wires through the holes of the smallest button and pushing the button up to the fold. Continue threading buttons onto the wire.

Stack the buttons to the size you desire, then make a single twist with the wire ends tight up against the last button to secure the stack. Thread the ends of the wire through the top of the basket lid. Use your fingers to twist the two wire ends together once.

Turn the lid upside down. Use the pliers to twist the wires together tightly. Trim the ends and push the cut ends against the basket lid.

Terry Taylor

Dem Bones, Dem Bones, Buttons

BRACELETS

Cut a 16-inch (40.6 cm) length of elastic beading cord. Fold the cord in half.

Thread a button on the two free ends, sliding it to the fold. Continue adding buttons until you have a stack of buttons that will almost encircle your wrist.

Add a silver focal bead to the stack of buttons and check the fit of the bracelet again.

Slide the button stack away from the folded end. Cut the cord to create two separate strands.

Knot opposite ends of the cord together carefully. After knotting, coat the knots with a small amount of clear nail polish. Let the polish dry.

Hide the knots inside the silver focal bead.

Watch Me Bloom Toy Box

Felt flowers on a canvas pop-up toy box have working button centers that youngsters can button and unbutton. When playtime is over, blooms can be stored neatly in the pocket located on one side of the box.

7½ yards (6.9 m) of green grosgrain ribbon, ⅜ inch (.95 cm) wide

Canvas pop-up toy box/bag, 14 inches square (35.6 cm)

Pencil

12 felt rectangles in various colors, 9 x 12 inches (22.9 x 30.5 cm) (this project used 3 hot pink, 3 lavender, 2 orange, 2 yellow, and 2 red)

Embroidery floss, 1 skein each in colors coordinating with your felt

18 two-hole yellow, orange, pink, and red buttons, 1⅛ inch (2.9 cm)

NOTE: This toy box has five flowers on three sides and a pocket on the fourth side. Create the flowers in any color combination you like or use the project photo as a guide.

Cut five lengths of grosgrain ribbon to make the flower stems. Position the ribbon on the bag/box as seen in the project photo. Use fabric glue or fusible webbing to attach the stems to the bag.

Cut five more lengths of ribbon and fold each into a "V." Place the fold at the bottom of each stem to create "grass blades." Glue them in place with fabric glue, leaving the ends free. Snip the ends at a sharp angle so they don't overlap.

Create a large circle pattern and use it to cut out five felt circles of various colors. Glue the circles at the top of each flower stem.

Double-thread a needle with six strands of floss and start stitching on the buttons from front to back. Stitch through one buttonhole and

Watch Me Bloom Toy Box

the center of the felt flower, and into the canvas bag. Bring the needle back through the other buttonhole. Tie the ends of the floss together in a tight double knot. Trim and fluff the ends to create the flower center.

Tie lengths of grosgrain ribbon into bows to make the leaves. Glue the bows at the knot, to the two longer stems.

Repeat the steps above to make five flowers with leaves and grass on two other sides of the box.

Fuse together two 9 x 12-inch (22.9 x 30.5 cm) hot pink felt rectangles, using the fusible web. Cut a strip of lavender felt and fuse it to the hot pink rectangle. Glue a length of ribbon to the center of the lavender strip, wrapping the ends. Evenly space and sew three buttons along the ribbon. Glue the pocket along the sides and the bottom edge.

Draw different flower patterns, using the project photo as a guide, and use them to cut out flowers in vari-ous colors to create the button-on felt flowers. Each pattern has a large and a small flower shape. Fuse two layers of the same-color felt together and cut out the large flower shape. Cut the corresponding smaller shape from a contrasting color and fuse it to the center of the larger flower shape.

Cut a 1¼-inch (3.2 cm) slit in the center of each flower for the but-tonhole, using sharp scissors. Use six strands of contrasting embroidery floss to add hand-running stitch details to each flower. Repeat to make fifteen flowers. Button the stitched flowers onto the bag.

Charger Clock

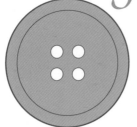

With a clock this fun, you'll truly enjoy watching time fly. Wooden toggles cleverly mark the quarter hours.

Sheet of fine grade sandpaper

Wooden charger plate, 11 or 12 inches (27.9 or 30.5 cm) in diameter

Rag or paper towel

Small foam paintbrush

Clear semi-gloss polyurethane

Power drill and ⅜-inch (9.5 mm) bit

40 to 50 assorted wood buttons in various sizes

Toothpicks (to apply glue)

Wooden beads

Clock quartz movement kit, for ½-inch-thick (1.3 cm) surfaces

AA battery

Sand down any rough spots on the charger plate. Clean off any residue with a damp rag or paper towel.

Use a foam paintbrush to apply a light coat of polyurethane to all sides of the plate. Allow to dry according to the manufacturer's directions.

Find the exact center of the plate, mark it with a pencil, and drill a hole. If necessary, sand any rough edges.

Arrange the buttons around the inner rim of the plate, deciding where the biggest buttons will go, then fill in the rest of the space with smaller buttons. If you want certain buttons to act as numbers on the clock, space them on the outer rim in the place of numbers.

Use white glue to attach the buttons. Allow the glue to sit and firm up. If there are any blank spaces, use small wooden beads as filler. Allow the piece to dry for at least 24 hours.

Check the back of the clock mechanism for the hanger—there is usually an indentation (possibly a hook) for hanging the clock. Once you've located the hanger, attach the clock mechanism to the back of the plate, making sure the section with the hanger is at the 12 o'clock position. Then attach the clock hands, add the battery, set the time and enjoy!

Barbra La Bosco

Sandy Snead

Attractive Magnets

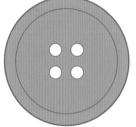

You're not alone if you felt an instant attraction to these magnets. With pleasing papers and eye-catching buttons, they're tiny works of art for the fridge…or the filing cabinet…or anywhere a magnet will go!

For each magnet:

Wood stain (optional)

Sponge brush

Wood disk (1½-inch and ¾-inch [3.8 cm and 1.9 cm] disks were used)

Wire cutters

Sandpaper

Large button, no bigger than 1¼ inches (3.2 cm)

Small button

Decorative paper

Circle craft punch

Small paintbrush

Gloss medium and varnish

Magnet

Stain both the sides and edges of the wood disk, if desired.

Clip shanks off using the wire cutters if any of the buttons have ring shanks. Sand any rough edges.

Sand the larger button down so that it lies as flat as possible on the wood disc. File down the smaller button so it sits evenly within the larger button.

Cut a circle out of the decorative paper using scissors or a craft punch. Use a paintbrush to apply a thin coat of the gloss medium and varnish to one side of the wood disk, then place the paper on the disk. Press firmly, then apply another coat of medium to the top and edge of the piece. Let it dry. Apply another coat if needed.

Adhere the magnet to the back of the wood disk with industrial strength glue. Place the disk on a flat surface and let it dry.

Glue the large button to the front of the disk, and then the small button to the large button. Place the piece on a flat surface to dry so the buttons do not slide off-center.

Freeform Embroidered Buttons

Dress up a ho-hum pillow with a touch of the exotic. Just one embroidered button can give a plain cushion the air of a Moroccan bazaar and serve as a festive focal point.

For each button cover:

¹⁄₁₆ yard (.06 m) of fabric*

Button template (from the back of the button packaging)

1 to 3 skeins embroidery thread, 2 strands each

Button cover kit

*Medium to lightweight fabrics should be used for these buttons.

Wash, dry, and iron the fabric, especially if you're planning to place buttons onto clothing or items that will be washed regularly.

Pin the template onto your fabric and cut it out. Trace the cutting line onto the wrong side of the fabric with a pencil, pen, or fabric marker.

Thread the needle with sewing thread, knotting it at one end. Sew running stitches along the interior circle, outlining the space of the button front within which you will sew. Place the stitches to the outside edge of your pencil line.

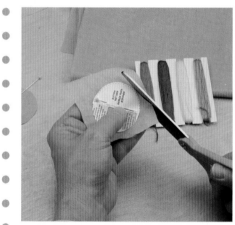

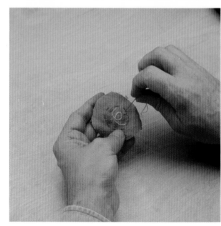

Caryn McCleskey

Freeform Embroidered Buttons

Create your design within the circular space outlined with sewing thread, referring to the project photo and using embroidery thread.

Clip the thread ends and remove the circular outline of running stitches after the embroidery is completed and knotted in back.

Sew running stitches approximately ¼ inch (6 mm) in from the outside edge of fabric to ease the centering of the design on the button. Place the button cover inside the circle and pull the thread to raise all the sides of the circle simultaneously.

Assemble following the manufacturer's directions and sew your button to a pillow.

Oh-So-Casual Rug

QUICK & EASY

It doesn't get much easier (or cuter!) than this jaunty rug—perfect for an entryway, the kids' room, or by the kitchen sink.

Mark the position of each button with a quilter's pin.

Use embroidery thread to stitch the buttons on.

Terry Taylor

Terry Taylor

Pyrographic Buttons

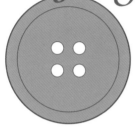

Got a burning desire to make your own buttons? You can create these sophisticated graphic buttons in a flash.

Wood button forms*

Drill and drill bit

Piece of scrap wood

Sandpaper

Pyrography tool and decorative tips

Clear acrylic wood finish or stain.

*Craft stores sell a wonderful array of wood shapes—ovals, squares, domes, and circles. Choose a shape and size that fits your button needs!

NOTE: practice makes perfect, so take the time (and use your scrap wood) to experiment with the pyrography tool.

Read the manufacturer's instructions before you use the tool. Experiment with different tips for different effects.

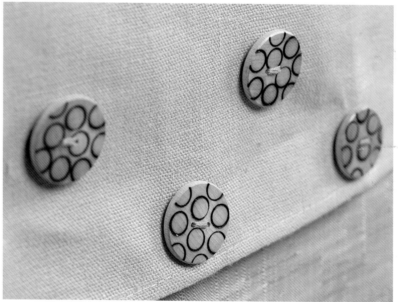

Pyrographic Buttons

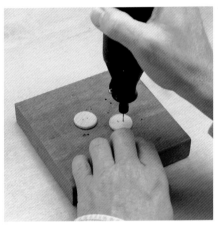  

Make two (or four) marks on each wood shape with a pencil to mark your buttonholes. Set one of the wood shapes on the piece of scrap wood when you drill your holes—this will prevent the back of your button from splintering. If needed, smooth any rough edges with the sandpaper. Set your drilled buttons aside.

Use the tool and selected tip to burn designs on the wood shapes. If desired, finish the buttons with a coat or two of acrylic wood finish or stain. Stitch the buttons in place.

QUICK & EASY

Snazzy Slipcover

Just as effectively as a slipcover changes the look of a couch or chair, buttons freshen up the look of a slipcover.

Use sturdy thread or embroidery floss to stitch a variety of buttons onto a slipcover.

Terry Taylor

Joan K. Morris

Dishtowel Placemats

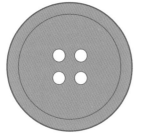

Whether today's menu features burgers and fries or rack of lamb, appetites will be whetted when the table is set with these fun button-edged placemats.

Dishcloth, at least 15 x 24 inches (38.1 x 61 cm)

Sewing machine

Fusible web for ironing seams together (optional)

Buttons in assorted colors and sizes, including single-hole buttons for the fringe

Embroidery floss in a color that matches the dishcloth, ½ skein per placemat

Fold the dishcloth in half, wrong sides together, so that you have a rectangle that's approximately 15 x 12 inches (38.1 x 30.5 cm). Press flat.

Machine-stitch all the way around the dishcloth, using matching thread, ¼ inch (6 mm) in from each edge, or use fusible web to iron the edges together.

Arrange the buttons to your satisfaction along the edges of the dishcloth. Stitch the buttons on using a doubled length of matching embroidery floss. Tie a knot under the button or run the floss to the next button, hiding it between the layers of the cloth. You can also stitch from the top of the button and tie off the floss at the top as a decoration.

Hide the knot under the edge of the cloth, then stitch through the cloth and through the button three times to make a button "fringe." To finish, tie a knot in the end, or run the floss through the cloth to the next button.

Celebratory Wreath

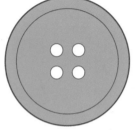

Easter, spring, and special birthdays are all reasons to celebrate. Hang this cheerful wreath anywhere and let it proclaim a warm welcome to family and friends.

Wire cutters

20-gauge copper wire

Approximately 25 large buttons

Vine wreath

28-gauge copper wire

Approximately 60 small buttons

Use the wire cutters to cut a 3-inch (7.6 cm) piece of the 20-gauge copper wire. Thread the wire through one of the large buttons. Repeat with four or five more of the large buttons, then twist the wires together so that the buttons form a floret.

Stick the floret into the wreath, and secure it with hot glue. Repeat these steps until the desired number of florets has been added to the wreath.

Use the wire cutters to cut an 18-inch (45.7 cm) piece of the 28-gauge copper wire. Thread the length of wire through 15 of the small buttons, then wrap the button wire around the wreath. Repeat these steps four times.

Cut a long enough piece of the 20-gauge copper wire to fill the inside of the wreath, then thread it through both large and small buttons. Bend the wire into the shape of the inside of the wreath, and secure it to the wreath with hot glue.

Skip Wade

The Buttonarium

The Buttonarium is an online button museum featuring hundreds of antique and collectible buttons. It features the private collection of button salesman Marc Jacobs and his button-collecting wife, Jennifer, who shared a passion for buttons long before they met.

Explore the Buttonarium's extensive virtual collection and you'll find buttons paying homage to beloved Hollywood stars, celebrated sports figures, and even popular cartoon characters. One particularly touching display showcases rare World War I locket buttons while another section features American Civil War era buttons, sure to please history buffs. Some of the more quirky buttons that can be found include classic cars, favorite cocktails, and a Playboy bunny logo button once sold as part of a blazer set!

With such a wide range of subject matter, the Buttonarium appeals to the button curious, the novice collector, and the button fanatic. Buttons are arranged by category, so it's easy to navigate—just choose a topic of interest and enjoy.

To search the vast archives of the Buttonarium, visit www.buttonarium.com. Says Jennifer Jacobs, "It is our work and our gift to the world."

From top to bottom:

Tintype Portrait Button
In 1906, the hottest ticket in town was getting your image on a tintype photograph button like this one. Although the button has evolved since then, the curiosity hasn't worn off.

World War I Locket Button
From the outside, these buttons are practically indistinguishable from the military-issue uniform buttons, but with a secret hinge mechanism, soldiers could slip pictures of their loved ones inside two small interior frames.

Man on the Moon Button
The Buttonarium features a whole cyber wing on space and space travel buttons. This particular button was part of a jasperware set created in 1976 to celebrate America's bicentennial.

World's Fair Button
The Buttonarium's collection of World's Fair buttons includes a button from the 1876 exhibition in Philadelphia. This particular button celebrates the 1933–1934 A Century of Progress International Exposition in Chicago.

White House Police Button
Sometimes buttons have a higher calling than mere fashion accessory. Adorning the likes of campus police to beat cops, uniform buttons such as these are brave little fasteners on a mission.

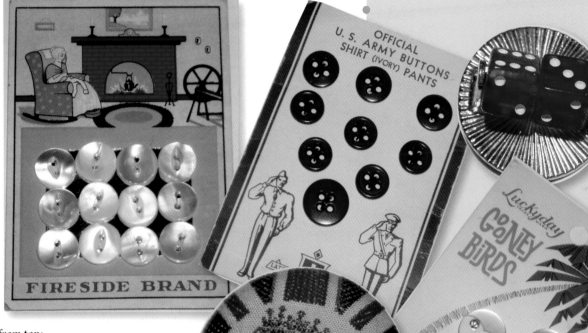

Clockwise from top:

Fireside Brand Button Card
Button cards, an exciting category of button collecting in their own right, are sometimes as charming as the buttons they hold. This card is one of many featured in the Buttonarium's collection.

U.S. Army Buttons
Keeping soldiers cozy and stylish, this vintage U.S. Army button card represents an interesting tidbit of military and button history.

Dice Button
This funky loop shank button features real moving dice, for games of chance on the go. While its age and original purpose are a mystery, this little number is a treat for any novelty button aficionado.

Gooney Birds
When they were first made, these funny little buttons only cost twenty-nine cents. With palm trees and odd bird bodies, this button card adds extra life and character to its buttons.

Fabric Coronation Button
From the early '50s, this unique button commemorates the coronation of Queen Elizabeth, just one sample from the Buttonarium's British Royalty wing (which they recommend enjoying with a cup of tea).

Reddy Kilowatt Buttons
Part fun and part propaganda, these hard-to-find Reddy Kilowatt buttons from the early '50s were used to promote electricity companies. With a light bulb nose and socket ears, Reddy is about as cute as a you know what.

Button Whimsy

Confetti Button Wall Quilt

Create a striking wall quilt with buttons, fused felt shapes, and a few simple decorative hand stitches. The right buttons—big, bold, and beautiful—can make this quilt come alive.

Fusible web and iron

9 squares of wool felt in assorted colors, each 8 inches (20.3 cm)

Rotary cutter (optional)

9 squares of black wool felt, each 6 inches (15.2 cm)

6-strand black embroidery floss

9 colorful decorative sew-on buttons, each 1⅜ inch (3.5 cm)

72 similar sew-on buttons in assorted colors (to match 8-inch felt squares), each ⅝ inch (1.6 cm)

Square of periwinkle wool felt, 24 inches (61 cm)

Square of black wool felt, 26 inches (66 cm)

Strip of black felt, 2½ x 22 inches (6.4 x 55 cm) (optional)

Apply the fusible web to the back of the 8-inch (20.3 cm) felt squares. From each square, cut two 2½-inch (6.4 cm) squares and several 1 x 3¾-inch (2.5 x 9.5 cm) rectangles.

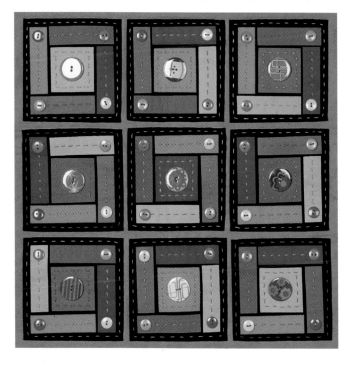

Pin a 2½-inch (6.4 cm) colored square in the middle of each 6-inch (15.2 cm) black square. Pin different colored rectangles around the central square, "log-cabin" style (see project

Confetti Button Wall Quilt

photo). Each quilt square should contain all five colors.

Arrange all nine quilt squares on a worktable. When the colors satisfy you, fuse the felt squares and rectangles to each black felt square. Trim the quilt blocks to 5¾ inches (14.6 cm) square.

Position a 1⅜-inch (3.5 cm) button at the center of each quilt block. Using six strands of embroidery floss, sew each button to the center of its quilt square. With the same color floss, add a row of hand-running stitches around all four sides of the center square.

Stitch a ⅝-inch (1.6 cm) button and a row of hand-running stitches to each side rectangle, using six strands of floss. Repeat this step for each rectangle in all nine quilt blocks.

Center the 24-inch (61 cm) periwinkle felt square over the 26-inch (66 cm) black felt square, leaving a 1-inch (2.5 cm) border on all sides. Use the fusible web to attach the two. Apply the fusible web to the top and bottom black felt border edges, fold them over, and trim the excess felt at the corners. Repeat for the left and right border edges.

Pin the quilt squares to the wall quilt, leaving about ¼ inch (6 mm) between each square. Centering the array should leave a 2-inch (5 cm) border of periwinkle at the edges. With the floss color used for the central buttons, attach each square to the wall quilt with hand-running stitches.

Use the black floss to stitch the remaining ⅝-inch (1.6 cm) buttons in the periwinkle border of the wall quilt. Position the buttons approximately 2 inches (5 cm) apart and about 1 inch (2.5 cm) from the edge of the black border.

Attach a 2½ x 22-inch (6.4 x 55 cm) strip of black felt to the back of the wall quilt for a hanging rod, if desired.

Elaine Schmidt

Terry Taylor

Buttoned-Down Cards

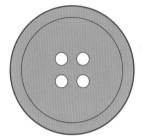

Vintage shirt-button cards are paired with grey pinstripe and pinked-edge shirting pattern papers to create these cards.

Decorative paper

Cardstock or purchased blank cards

Decorative edge scissors

Shirt-button cards

Cut a piece of background paper slightly smaller than the dimensions of the front of your card. Adhere it to the card with spray adhesive.

Use decorative edge scissors to cut out a piece of paper somewhat larger than your shirt-button card. Adhere the paper to the card.

Glue the shirt-button card to the card. Then add decorative stitching to the card, or any other embellishment that strikes your fancy.

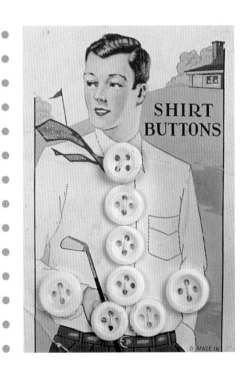

Clown Troupe

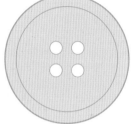

Stacking buttons in a variety of shapes, colors, and sizes, you can create stick-figure toys that can assume personalities and characteristics of almost anyone. Is this how Barbie got her start?

Per button man:

36 inches of black waxed thread

Assorted buttons in a variety of sizes and colors

Cut two 18-inch (45.7 cm) lengths of the black waxed thread.

Line up the buttons, on a flat surface, in the shape of a man (see project photo). From the bottom of one of the "foot buttons," run one end of thread through the hole of each button (or opposite holes if there are four). Even out the ends of the thread, so the button rests in the center. Repeat with the other foot button. These are the two leg pieces.

Stack the leg buttons above the feet by running the two ends of the thread through each button. For four-hole buttons, run the thread only through the two opposite holes so the buttons stay lined up. When you reach the top of the leg, tie a single knot. Repeat for the other leg.

String the midsection by running both strings from each leg through one of the holes of the larger buttons. Repeat until you are one button or two buttons from the top of the midsection. Separate one string from each hole and lay them to the side for the arms. Run the remaining two center strings through the last midsection button and tie a single knot.

String the two side threads through the arm buttons, going through only one hole, to the last button, then string them back to the midsection using the other hole. Wrap the remaining thread from both arms around the center strings and tie a double knot between the midsection buttons.

Thread the two strings through the neck buttons and the head buttons, then the hat buttons. Tie a double knot at the top. Tie the excess thread in a knot above the hat for hanging.

Joan K. Morris

Toggle Button Seals

Seal your correspondence with more than just a quick lick. Heralding from the days of kings and noblemen, seals have long provided panache to letters and invitations.

For each seal:

Decorative button (for making impressions)

Toggle button (for the handle)

Piece of shoestring leather, 12 inches (30.5 cm) long

Wax for the seal or hot glue made for seals

Assorted paper

Spray lubricant or cooking spray (to keep the buttons from sticking in the hot glue)

Small paintbrush

Inkpads (optional)

Paper towel

NOTE: If using wax, you can choose a button with more detail as wax shows fine details better. If you use hot glue instead, choose a button with less detail.

Use clear industrial glue to attach the decorated button to the toggle button, following the manufacturer's instructions. Let the pieces dry overnight. Thread the piece of leather through the toggle button and tie the end in a knot.

To use wax: Drip wax on the paper so that it forms a puddle, then place the button in the wax, following the manufacturer's instructions. Let the piece sit a few seconds, then gently remove the button using a rocking motion.

To use hot glue: Choose your paper keeping in mind that the paper color may show through if you're using hot glue. Following the manufacturer's instructions, drip the hot glue on the paper in a puddle, then wait 1 to 2 minutes. Meanwhile, lightly coat your chosen button with spray lubricant or cooking spray. Press the button into the glue, let it sit for a few seconds, and then gently remove it using a rocking motion.

TIP: If you want to show more detail on the impression, use a paintbrush or your finger to lightly apply ink to the wax or hot glue impression. Wipe off any excess ink with a paper towel.

Susan Gower

Keepsake Box Trio

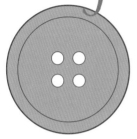

No matter the size or shape, you can make any box a special trove for treasures by artfully covering it in buttons. For a more mod look, choose bold hues in the latest color trends and apply the buttons randomly.

For each box:

Papier-mâché craft box

Felt

Small paintbrush

White buttons

White sand

Use a pencil to trace a template around the bottom of the box onto a sheet of paper. Use the template to cut a piece from the felt—it will be used later for finishing the bottom of the box.

Paint one side of the box with a layer of all-purpose white glue, then add buttons in your desired pattern. Sprinkle a fine layer of the white sand onto the side of the box while the glue is still tacky. Remove the excess sand and allow the glue to dry overnight.

Repeat the steps above for the remaining sides of the box. After covering the sides and the lid of the box, glue the felt that you cut out in the first step to the bottom of the box.

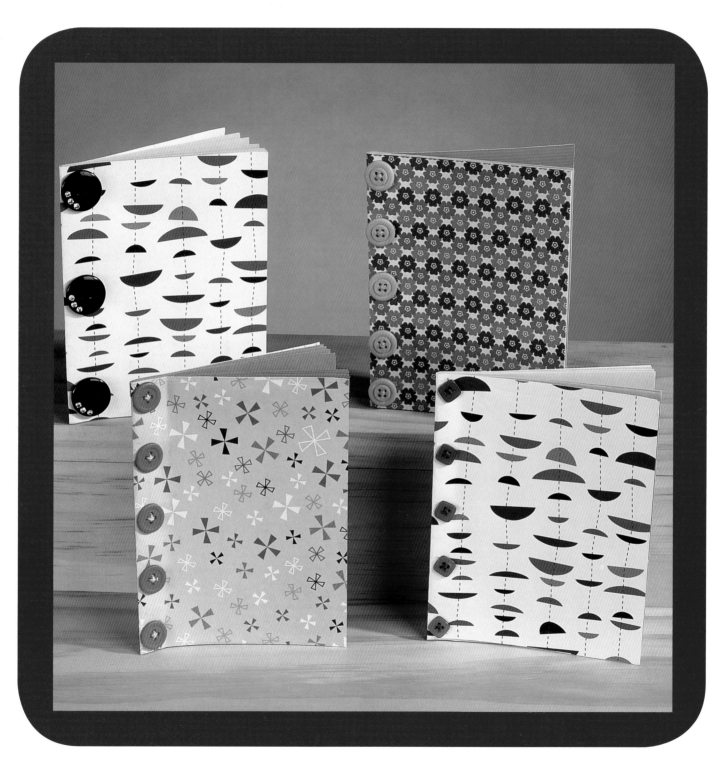

Diane Baker

Button-Bound Books

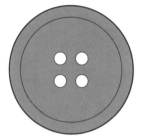

Use your favorite paper, some colorful buttons, and a few spare minutes to create a special four or eight-page button-bound book. They make great mini photo albums, travel journals, or special-occasion mementos.

Per book:

1 or 2 sheets of 24–80 lb. paper, 8½ x 11 inches (21.6 x 27.9 cm)*

Bone folder (optional)

Sheet of plain or patterned 40–100 lb. cardstock, 8½ x 5½ inches (21.6 x 13.8 cm)

Clear adhesive tape (optional)

3 large paperclips or binder clips

3 to 5 sew-through buttons, ½ to ¾ inch (1.3 to 1.9 cm) in diameter

Thimble

Paper cutter or craft knife

Cutting mat (or an old magazine)

*A four-page book requires one sheet of paper; an eight-page book uses two sheets.

Make a light crease as a guide, then fold the 24–80 lb. sheet(s) in half, short sides together. Line up the edges, then flatten the fold with a bone folder or pencil for a professional appearance.

Repeat the previous step and fold the sheet(s) in half again, this time in the other direction. The last folded edge will become the bound edge of your book.

Fold the cardstock sheet in half, short sides together. Press the crease and slip it over the interior sheets, folded sides together. To further pro-tect the book, you can add a strip of tape inside the binding edge of the back cover. Secure the three open sides with paper clips.

Mark where the buttons will line up by drawing a light pencil line ¼ inch (6 mm) from the top and bot-tom of the book, perpendicular to the binding edge. Along the binding edge, measure 2⅝ inches (6.67 cm) in from either line. Lightly mark this point in pencil.

Button-Bound Books

Place the first button at the pencil mark so its outside rim almost hits the binding edge. Pre-punch the paper through the buttonholes. Thread the needle with doubled thread, knotted at the end. Using the thimble, pull the first stitch from the front to the back.

Stitch the buttons onto the book, going through the holes three or four times to secure the button. When you come up through the paper for the last stitch, do not go through the buttonhole. Pull the needle under the button, catching the thread, and tie a firm knot.

Remove the paper clip from the top edge. On a cutting mat, carefully trim that edge along the pencil line with a paper cutter or craft knife and ruler. Cut in a single stroking motion, pressing firmly to cut through every layer of paper. Replace the clip and repeat to trim the bottom edge. If necessary, trim the front edge of the book.

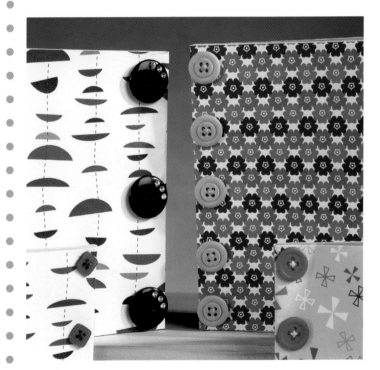

Quick & Easy Adorned Scrapbook Pages

Scrapbooking is a labor of love and an expression of your inner self. Use buttons as graphic elements on your pages, or to emphasize and accent an existing design.

Stitch or glue buttons to your scrapbook layout for additional depth, texture, and interest. Use single or stacked to frame a photo, attach other elements to the page, or to highlight text.

 Erikia Ghumm

Diane Baker

Simple Buttonhole Note Cards

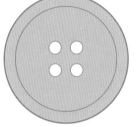

A pretty buttoned-up notecard lends your message a bit of mystery and intrigue. The contrasting strip of paper decorates and reinforces the edge of the card for the button closure.

Per note card:

Sheet of 20–60 lb. paper, 8½ x 5½ inches (21.6 x 14 cm)

2 contrasting strips of 20–60 lb. paper, 1 x 5½ inches (2.5 x 14 cm)

Button, no larger than ¾ inch (20 mm), with 2 to 4 holes

Cutting mat (or old magazine)

Craft knife

Fold the sheet of paper in half to make a 4¼x 5½-inch (10.8 x 14 cm) card. Press the fold with a pencil.

Use a glue stick to attach one of the contrasting strips of paper to the front edge of the notecard, using the project photo as a guide for placement.

Place the card face down and rub it with the side of a pencil to make sure the strip is adhered.

Glue the other strip of paper to the inside edge of the notecard, using the same process as above. Allow the notecard to dry.

Center the button on the front strip of the notecard and make light pencil marks on either side of the button at its widest diameter.

Open the card and place it face up on the cutting mat. Use a craft knife to cut a rectangular buttonhole. Check to be sure that the button passes easily through the hole; enlarge it if needed.

Center the button on the strip of paper on top of the buttonhole. With the sewing needle, lightly mark the sewing holes of the button on the inside of the card, through the holes.

Thread the needle with a double-strand of thread. Gently sew on the button, hiding the knot underneath.

Elegant Packages

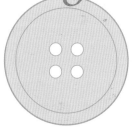

These packages are so pretty, don't be surprised if the recipient is reluctant to open them. Monochrome buttons accompanied by feathers, pleats, and ribbons guarantee a stunning presentation.

Gift Boxes

Gift box

Glossy white wrapping paper

Invisible tape

Roll of white ribbon, ¼ inch (6 mm) wide

White shell buttons of various sizes (some with side holes, some with shanks, depending upon which package embellishment you've chosen)

Gift Bag

22-gauge wire

Wire cutters

Round and rectangular shell buttons

Glass pearl beads

Glossy white gift bag

White feather fringe

White satin ribbon

GIFT BOX

Wrap the box carefully in the white wrapping paper. Seal it with invisible tape.

Cut a length of ribbon and thread one end onto an embroidery needle. Using the project photograph as a guide, arrange your buttons and run a needle through the shanks or holes of the buttons. Use a toothpick to add a drop of white glue to secure them.

Wrap the button-covered ribbon on the box and secure the ends with a simple bow or knot.

GIFT BAG

Cut three 6-inch (15.2 cm) pieces of wire. Stack your buttons and beads and then run one of the wire lengths up through the stack. Thread the wire back down through the stack and twist it tightly. Make three button stacks.

Twist the wired ends of all three button stacks together.

Make a circle with the feathers and hot-glue them on the bag. Glue the wire-wrapped buttons in the center of the feather fringe.

Embellish with ribbon.

Joan K. Morris

Joan K. Morris

112

Baroque Holiday Tree

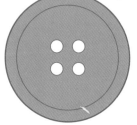

Think of it as portable elegance. This button-packed topiary will make a glittering decorating statement on a mantel, dining room table, or anywhere else it's placed.

Wooden candleholder, 5 inches (12.7 cm) tall

Gold spray paint

Polystyrene foam tree form, 12 inches (30.5 cm) tall

Paintbrush

Black water-based paint*

125 gold, black, white, and red buttons in assorted sizes

2 matching flower-shaped buttons

Wire cutters

Box of pearl-headed corsage pins

*If you want to cover some of the tree form's texture, use a paint made for covering polystyrene foam.

Paint the candleholder with gold spray paint and the foam form with the black paint. Let both pieces dry.

Place the candleholder in the center bottom of the tree form and push about an inch of it into the form until a hole is made. Hot-glue the candleholder in place.

Decorate the tree by placing a small dab of hot glue on the back of each button and firmly pushing it into place on the form. Try to cover all the space on the tree form.

Add the two matching flower-shaped buttons at the top of the tree. First use wire cutters to cut the shanks off so that the backs are flat. Hot-glue them back-to-back and then attach them to the top of the tree.

Fill in any open areas with corsage pins. When placing the pins at the top of the tree, aim them down so that they don't come out the other side.

Sandy Snead

Wall Flowers

These delightful wallflowers aren't shy and retiring in the least—they're bold botanical additions to any décor.

Foam core board

Wood picture frame

Background fabric (suede is shown)

Double-sided tape

Wool felt

Buttons of your choice

6-strand embroidery floss

Awl or heavy needle

Needle-nose pliers

Cut a piece of the foam core to fit inside the frame. Make sure you allow room for the background fabric to wrap around the edges. This will be your base.

Cut a piece of the background fabric that's slightly larger than the base.

Place strips of double-sided tape around the edge of the back side of the base. Wrap the fabric around the base front-to-back and secure to the tape.

Use a pencil to sketch a simple flower shape on the sheet of paper. Using the sketch as a template, cut flower petals and leaves out of the wool felt, then use fabric glue to adhere them to the background.

Glue the buttons to the flower centers.

Use three strands of the embroidery floss to add decorative stitches like running stitches or French knots for stems and details on or around the flower.

Button Monograms

Spice up your monogram with a host of colorful buttons.
Add a few rhinestones if you'd like some sparkle.

Spray paint wooden letters with your desired color.

Arrange and then glue down a variety of buttons on the letters. Fill in any gaps between the buttons with rhinestones.

Erikia Ghumm

Fanciful Bouquet

Nothing says "Happy Birthday," "Get Well Soon," or "Congratulations" like flowers. These Seuss-like blooms are so full of exuberance that you'll want to pluck a posy of them to give as well as to keep.

Buttons in assorted colors and shapes, ¼ to 1½ inches (6.4 mm to 3.8 cm)

Wire cutters

22-gauge green floral wire

Pliers

Green floral tape

Assorted green print, floral, and striped decorative papers

Laminating sheets

Hole punch, ⅛ inch (3 mm)

Create stacks of button "petals" arranging from smallest to largest.

Use the wire cutters to snip a 24-inch (61 cm) piece of green floral wire for each flower. Fold the piece in half.

Fanciful Bouquet

Run the wire through the shank or the holes of the top (smallest) button, positioning the button at the fold. Thread the wire through the rest of the button stack. Tip: When adding a button with four holes, thread the wire through two holes that are diagonal from each other.

Twist the two lengths of wire together tightly under the last button in each flower, using pliers to make the twist secure. Continue twisting the wire lengths together until you reach the end.

Wrap the wire in green floral tape to form a stem, starting at the top of the wire, under the last button in the blossom.

Create a leaf template on white paper. With a pencil, trace the pattern onto the backside of two different pieces of decorative paper. Fold the decorative paper so the right sides are together and trace the template onto the back. Cut out the leaves (you should now have two pieces), and stack them so the right sides are facing out. Glue them together with a glue stick.

Cut out another leaf that is ½ inch (1.3 cm) smaller then the original leaf, if desired. Stack the smaller leaf on top of the larger ones, and laminate.

Use the hole punch to make a hole at the end of the laminated leaf. Thread the covered stem through the hole and run the leaf up the stem until it rests beneath the button blossom. Add a second leaf in the same fashion.

Wrap floral tape around the stem under the leaves three or four times to hold the leaves in place.

Joan K. Morris

Terry Taylor

Big Button Pulls

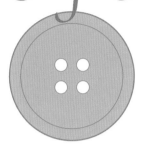

The lively color and bold concave shape of these oversized buttons inspired this unique drawer treatment.

Small unfinished wooden box
with drawers

Paint formulated for wood

Large buttons

Drill and drill bit

Sandpaper

Copper craft wire

Wire cutters

Pliers

Paint the box a color that matches or sharply contrasts with the color of your buttons. Hold one of the buttons in place on the drawer and mark the holes on the drawer. Remove the button and drill holes in the drawer.

Use the sandpaper to sand a small area on the back of the button. Sanding it flat creates a better fit, so that the button adheres to the drawer.

Mix a small amount of two-part epoxy following the manufacturer's instructions. Apply the epoxy to the flat area of the button and place it on the drawer. Take care to match the holes in the button with the holes you drilled in the drawer. Allow the epoxy to cure.

Cut a length of wire approximately 12 inches (30.5 cm) in length. Use the wire to "stitch" the button in place. Start from the inside of the drawer, leaving a small tail of wire. Thread the wire several times through the holes, then use the pliers to twist the two wire ends together. Trim the twisted ends and push them up against the inside of the drawer.

Playful Tassels

Like the cherry atop of a sundae, tassels add the finishing touch to almost any item. Add a color coordinated button tassel to a ceiling fan pull, window shade, or pillow for a pop of pizzazz.

For each tassel:

Skein of embroidery floss in a color that matches the buttons

Piece of cardboard, 2 x 4 inches (5 x 10.2 cm)

18 inches (45.7 cm) of thin ribbon, in a color that matches the buttons

7 to 12 assorted buttons

Wrap the embroidery floss around the piece of cardboard 30 times. Run the piece of ribbon under the embroidery floss and up to the top of the cardboard, centering it under the embroidery floss, making sure both ends are equal lengths.

Tie the ribbon tightly in a square knot around the embroidery floss, then slide the tied floss off of the cardboard. Cut the floss at the opposite end from the knot. Take another piece of embroidery floss and wrap it around the strands just below the knot. Tie a knot in the floss and hide the ends.

Arrange the buttons in a stack. Thread one end of the ribbon through the embroidery needle. Run the needle and ribbon up through one side of the buttonholes and out the top. Repeat for the other end of the ribbon except run it up through the other side of the buttonholes. Tie a knot in the ribbon at the top of the buttons and then another knot 4 inches (10.2 cm) further up the ribbon. Trim the ribbon end.

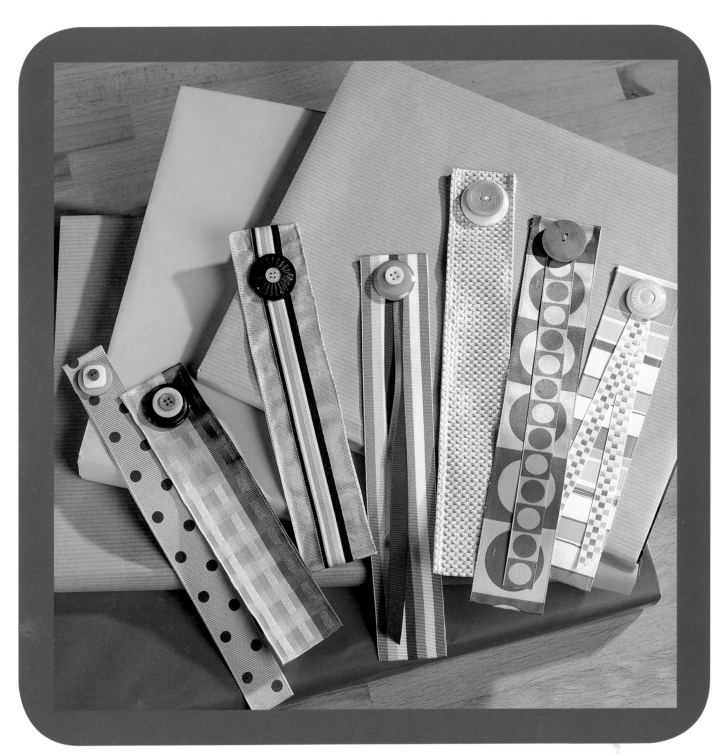

Barbra La Bosco

Ribbon Bookmarks

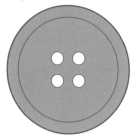

Ever find yourself marking your place in a book with a piece of junk mail, a scrap of paper, or even (heaven forbid!) resorting to dog-earring? When it's time to shut off the light, tuck one of these attractive ribbon bookmarks between the pages.

Per bookmark:

½ yard (.46 m) of wire-trimmed or stiff grosgrain ribbon, 1 to 2 inches (2.5 to 5 cm) wide

Assorted buttons, preferably not shank buttons

Cut the ribbon to the length of your choice. This will serve as the base bookmark. With the ribbon lying flat in front of you, fold each end under ½ inch (1.3 cm), then press the folds firmly so that creases are formed. Open up each crease and apply fabric glue. Fold the creases inward and press them firmly for a couple of seconds so that a sticky contact is made.

Fold the entire ribbon in half until the glued edges meet and press a crease at the center fold. Then open the ribbon and apply fabric glue to one half of the piece. Fold the ribbon in half and press it.

Glue on additional ribbons, if desired, then stack and glue buttons on top of the ribbon ends. To give the appearance of the button stack being stitched to the bookmark, sew through the holes on the top button before gluing it to the stack.

Orb Ornaments

No sewing, no glue, no hassle; just a box of pins and a bunch of buttons. Pinning on the buttons is fun, creative, and therapeutic. Gather family and friends to join in and the holiday tree will be adorned in no time.

For each ornament:

14-inch (35.6 cm) piece of ribbon, ⅛ inch (3.2 cm) wide

Polystyrene foam ball, 3 inches (7.6 cm) in diameter

120 or more buttons, in assorted sizes and colors

70 or more color-headed or pearl-headed corsage pins

Make a ribbon hanger by pinning each end of the ribbon side by side so that a loop is formed for hanging.

Cover the entire foam ball evenly in stacks of one, two, or three buttons, attaching each stack with one or more pins. Overlap some of the edges of the buttons for better coverage and added visual interest.

Make a larger stack of buttons at the bottom of the ball, if desired.

Joan K. Morris

Button Collecting for Beginners

Button collecting can be a fascinating hobby, and chances are you can start right at home. A fabulous button collection may be as nearby as your kitchen junk drawer! After you've mined the depths of your personal button reserves (and maybe those of a few willing relatives), here are some tips to help you expand your collection:

There's a great big world of buttons out there so pick a style, color, material, or subject to focus on. Maybe enameled buttons are your thing. Or buttons depicting space and space travel. The possibilities are endless but keep in mind that some types of buttons, like presidential inauguration buttons, antique, or specialty buttons, can be quite rare… and quite expensive.

How does one go about expanding a fledgling collection? Try yard sales, estate sales, button shows, or specialty button Web sites. You never know what you'll find, and that's half the fun. You just might luck into a priceless collection waiting inside a yard sale grab bag.

A few standard supplies—like a toothbrush, a polishing cloth, and baby or mineral oil—make button restoration a snap. Armed with a button price guide from your local library or bookstore, you'll know exactly what your little treasures are worth.

If it seems you have a natural affinity for button collecting, take your act on the road. Founded in 1938, the National Button Society organizes annual button collecting competitions. Or share your passion by joining a button-collecting club; field trips to button conventions and button museums will keep you in the know.

Once you've begun your collection, you'll want to show it off. While mason jars are an obvious storage choice, why hide all those beauties? Try sewing your buttons onto display cards in unique patterns (like Frieda Warther, on the facing page) or creating one of the craft projects featured in this book, but be sure not to ruin any of your prized collectibles!

Warther Carvings Museum & Button Collection

Dover, Ohio

When Henry Ford offered Ernest Warther $75,000 cash plus $5,000 a year to move his family to Ford's Greenfield Village as a living exhibit, Warther declined. Reportedly, he told Ford that his roof didn't leak, he wasn't hungry, and his wife Freida "had all her buttons"—a reference to her staggering collection of 73,282 buttons. Freida's collection remains in the house they shared, in the small town of Dover, Ohio, and is displayed exactly as she sewed them, on display boards in intricate designs.

At the age of 10, Freida became captivated by buttons and proceeded to collect them for the next 73 years. She collected every kind of button, from brass to pearl and everything in between, and eventually amassed over 100,000 of the little fasteners. One of the most special buttons in her collection includes a button from Mrs. Lincoln's inaugural address!

Once her children were grown, Freida started displaying her buttons in geometric patterns on the walls and ceiling of her button house. She drew inspiration from quilting patterns and carefully hand-stitched her button arrangements onto fabric panels, by hand. The result is simply stunning, and quite dizzying!

For more information, visit www.roadsideamerica.com/attract/OHDOVwarther. html.

Designers

DIANE BAKER is a lifelong crafter, artist, writer, and designer, who can't resist any medium—she has even made jewelry out of the bands used for braces! Diane is the author of the beading book *Jazzy Jewelry to Make and Wear* (Williamson Publishing, 2000). She lives in Seattle, Washington, with her husband, two teen-aged daughters, and a large fluffy dog (who doubles as her personal trainer).

CANDIE COOPER started making jewelry in high school and hasn't stopped since. Her passion lies in designing jewelry from unique materials in vibrant colors. She's the author of *Felted Jewelry* (2007, Lark Books) and co-author of *Designer Needle Felting* (2007, Lark Books). Her jewelry has been exhibited throughout the United States, England, and Europe. Today you can find her working and teaching from her studio in Shenzhen, China. Visit her website at www.candiecooper.com.

ERIKIA GHUMM is a nationally known artist, author, and instructor. Her work has been published in craft magazines and books, and she has authored/coauthored two books, *Tags Reinvented: New Approaches to Creating Scrapbook Tags*, and *Montage Memories: Creating Altered Scrapbook Pages*, both from Memory Makers Books. Erikia has appeared on HGTV and the DIY Network. Visit her website at www.erikiaghumm.com.

SUSAN GOWER is a freelance artist who lives in Barrington, Rhode Island. She studied at the Rhode Island School of Design but is primarily a self-taught artist. In addition to creating hand-crafted pincushions and button boxes, Susan deals in vintage trims and buttons through her business, Nifty Thrifty Dry Goods.

ELIZABETH HOOPER lives in Chicago with her boyfriend and their mini-menagerie of three cats and two dogs. Elizabeth has been crafting since childhood, and her repertoire of skills includes sewing, knitting, embroidery, painting, and photography. To see more of Elizabeth's work, check out her online shop, loosestringetsy.com, and her crafting blog, squeakywheel.motime.com.

Throughout her life, **BARBRA LA BOSCO** has engaged in many creative activities, including knitting, needlepoint, and crocheting. She majored in art in college and taught professionally for more than 33 years. Creating and playing with buttons is one of Barbra's favorite artistic outlets. Now retired, she is always on the hunt for new buttons and projects, and often purchases clothing or home decorations just because of the buttons they feature. Buttons talk to her! Barbra sells her pins, clocks, bookmarks, and other pieces privately and online at www.allaboutthe-buttons.etsy.com.

CARYN MCCLESKEY is a part-time designer and crafter, who commutes to her day job in Washington, DC. She designs and creates items for sale at local shows, along with embellishing clothing and making gifts for family and friends. The constraints of commuting and a desire to redesign, repurpose, and reuse common items often inspire her designs and creations. Current projects involve hand-sewing, machine-sewing, embroidery, decoupage, collage, repurposing used books, and decorating.

The artistic endeavors of **JOAN K. MORRIS** have led her down many successful creative paths, including costume design for motion pictures, and ceramics. Joan has contributed projects to numerous Lark books, including *Hardware Style, Hip Handbags, Beaded Home, Tops to Sew, Pillows to Sew, Curtains to Sew*, and many more.

Award-winning designer and product development consultant **ELAINE SCHMIDT** works with a wide variety of manufacturers to conceive, develop, and promote new products in the craft industry. She teaches and demonstrates across the country and has appeared on several TV shows. Her upscale designs are featured in new product lines and packaging, books, magazines, advertisements, showrooms, and project sheets. Elaine specializes in fabric, fiber, and embellishment crafts and is always looking for new ways to make crafting projects fun, easy, and stylish.

SANDY SNEAD is a mixed media artist based in Charlotte, North Carolina. After graduating with a B.F.A. in graphic design, she decided she was in the wrong field. She found her calling after taking a jewelry-making class. Over the years, she has designed jewelry while working in the areas of visual display and textile design. The desire to play with different media eventually led her into collage work. This element quickly found its way into her jewelry designs. Sandy enjoys digging through piles of old buttons and other items at flea markets, searching for pieces that may be used in her creations. You can see more of her work at www.adorn-bysandy.com.

ANDREA STERN of Chauncey, Ohio, grew up surrounded by family members who made art in one form or another. Her own artistic endeavors started with simple drawings and quickly progressed to painting, beadwork, and quilting. She received a formal degree in art history in 1990. She now owns a bead business that allows her to apply the principles of design that she learned in school. Examples of her work are available at www.embellishmentcafe.com or andibeads.blogspot.com.

TERRY TAYLOR is an acquisitions editor at Lark Books. He's the author of several books including *Altered Art* (2004, Lark), *Artful Paper Dolls* (2006, Lark), and *The Altered Object* (2006, Lark). He's a jeweler in his spare time and prefers to spend his vacation time taking metalworking classes. His other passion requires him to fly around the country to see well-known opera companies perform.

Asheville, North Carolina, is home for **SKIP WADE**, a freelance photo stylist and designer. His work has appeared in a number of Lark books.

Index

Adhesives, 10

Basics, 9

Bone buttons, 68

Button King, 48

Buttonarium, 90

Collecting, 128

Decoupage, 40

Embroidery, 78

History, 11

Jewelry, 14, 30, 36, 46, 70

Patchwork, 43

Pyrography, 83

Quick & Easy, 29, 33, 81, 85, 107

Quilt, 93

Sewing, 11

Shell buttons, 26

Sizes, 9

Toolbox, 10

Types, 9

Warther Carvings Museum, 129

Wheat pennies, 23

Wire cutters, 13